Jeffery Foust

Okinawa Travel Guide 2024

A Complete Guide to Unforgettable Adventures, Rich Heritage, Reliable Recommendations and Insider Tips for an Enthralling Journey to Japan

Copyright © 2023 Jeffery Foust

All Right Reserved

No part of this publication may be reproduced, distributed, or transmitted in any form or by any means, including photocopying, recording, or other electronic or mechanical methods, without the prior written permission of the author, except in the case of brief quotations embodied in critical reviews and specific other noncommercial uses permitted by copyright law.

This publication is protected by copyright law and international treaties. Unauthorized reproduction or distribution of this publication, or any portion of it, may result in severe civil and criminal penalties and will be prosecuted to the maximum extent possible under the law.

Every effort has been made to ensure that the contents of this publication are accurate and up-to-date. However, the author makes no warranties or representations, express or implied, regarding the information's completeness, accuracy, or reliability.

The views and opinions expressed in this publication are those of the author and do not necessarily reflect any agency or organization's official policy or position.

Table of Contents

Table of Contents 3
Introduction 7
Brief History of Okinawa 13
What is Okinawa most famous for? 17
Top tips to know before you go to Okinawa 19
Getting There 22
Accommodations 24
Transportation 28
    Renting a Car 28
    Bus 31
    Okinawa Urban Monorail 34
    Taxi 35
Language Tips 36
    Basic Phrases 36
    Language Apps 37
What to Pack to Okinawa 41
Things to Do in Okinawa 42
Must-Visit Destinations 49
    Naha 49
    Northern Okinawa 56

    Ishigaki 59

    Miyako 64

Traditional Okinawan Arts 67

    Eisa Dance 67

    Sanshin Music 69

Culinary Delights 72

    Okinawan Cuisine 72

    Popular Local Dishes 75

    Popular Restaurant to dine in Okinawa 78

Outdoor Adventures 82

    Snorkeling and Diving 82

    Hiking and Nature Trails... 86

Events and Festivals 89

    Naha Matsuri 89

    Shurijo Castle Festival 92

    Orion Beer Festival... 95

Weather and Climate 98

Best Times to Visit 102

Currency and Payment Methods 104

Health and Safety Information 107

Entertainment and Nightlife 111

Conclusion 115

An Open Letter from the Author

Dear Readers,

I am delighted to present to you the "*Okinawa Travel Guide 2024*," your premier companion to the captivating paradise of Okinawa, Japan. As you grasp this guide in your hands, you embark on a journey of exploration, adventure, and unmatched beauty.

Whether you acquired this guide to streamline the planning of your upcoming Okinawa trip or to discern if Okinawa is an ideal destination for your next vacation, I commend you for taking this crucial first step. You are part of an exclusive 1% who seek out life's most exceptional experiences.

Okinawa unfolds as a treasury of natural marvels, cultural opulence, and countless opportunities for indelible experiences. This guide serves as your passport to uncovering every facet of this extraordinary island, from its verdant landscapes and cascading waterfalls to its unspoiled beaches and thriving communities.

Considerable dedication has gone into crafting this guide to ensure you possess the most current, authentic, and comprehensive information essential for an extraordinary experience on this enchanting island.

Warm Regards,

Jeffery Foust

Jeffery Foust,

Travel-Expert

Introduction

Okinawa, Japan's southernmost prefecture, is a chain of islands with its own history as an independent kingdom, a distinctly subtropical climate, and the birthplace of karate. Visit magnificent beaches and coastlines with an amazing array of coral and undersea life, as well as the ruins and restored castles of the Ryukyu kings. Come for whale watching and dragon boat races, as well as rare flora and fauna and an island mindset that allows you to forget the clock and follow the sun.

Mention Okinawa to a mainland Japanese and you'll almost certainly get a wistful sigh in response. Warm weather all year, clear seas teeming with fish, fantastic food, gentle people, unspoiled beaches and jungle...the list goes on. More than a hundred subtropical islands, known collectively as the Ryky Shot, stretch over 700 kilometers of ocean from Kysh southwest to Yonaguni-jima, almost within sight of Taiwan, and are one of Japan's favorite getaways.

Okinawa's lush vegetation, postcard-perfect beaches, and world-class coral reefs can entice even the most jaded traveller - if you've had your fill of shrines and temples and want to check out some of Japan's best beaches and dive sites, or simply fancy a spot of winter sun, then Okinawa is well worth a visit.

The largest island in the group, Okinawa-Hont, also known simply as Okinawa, serves as the region's transportation hub and is home to the prefectural capital, Naha. It is also the most populous and developed of the Ryūkyū chain, owing in large part to the controversial presence of American military bases. Okinawa-Hontō is rich in historical sites, many of which are associated with the Battle of Okinawa at the end of the Pacific War. However, the island has more to offer than battle sites, particularly in its northern region, where the old way of life can still be found in isolated villages.

If you want to experience the best of the area, you'll need to take a plane or ferry to explore the dozens of outlying islands off the coast of Okinawa, many of which are uninhabited. Not far from Naha, you'll find beautiful beaches and some of the best dive spots near the Kerama islands (just 30km from Okinawa-Hontō). Divers and beach aficionados will want to visit the islands of Miyako (Miyako-jima) and Ishigaki (Mishaki-jima), which are located in the lower part of the Okinawa chain. If you're after an idyllic getaway, you can't go wrong with the island of Taketomi. But if you're an adventurer, you'll want to explore the island of Iriomote, which is covered in thick mangrove and steaming rainforest and is home to the Iriomote Lynx.

On these outer islands, you will also find the strongest manifestation of the much-heralded culture of Ryūkyū, which was born of contacts with Taiwan and China as well as with other parts of Japan. The most visible manifestations of this culture can be found in the cuisine and the use of colour and tropical patterns. The Chinese influence can also be seen in the architecture, traditional clothing and the martial arts of karate, which is the preferred form of protection for the warriors of the region. Shaman (also known as yuta) keeps ancient religious beliefs alive. Sumo bouts between bulls are held in the center of Okinawa-Hoto. There are dozens of variations of the local dialect, as well as unique musical instruments and a unique musical style that has been embraced by international audiences through bands such as Nēnēs, Diamantes, Champloose and others.

If you're lucky, you may stumble upon a local celebration, like enormous rope tug-of-war competitions or dragon-boat races. However, the most significant yearly occasion is the Eisā festival, which takes place on the fifteenth day of the seventh lunar month. During this event, individuals completely surrender to the ceaseless beats of drums, flutes, and the three-stringed sanshin.

Other than Hokkaidō, Okinawa is home to the majority of Japan's pristine natural areas and highest biodiversity.

The warm Kuroshio Current, which sweeps up the east coast and promotes coral reef growth, is largely responsible for the abundance of underwater life that makes up this ecosystem. However, there are also several endemic species found on land, such as the yamaneko, Iriomote's wild cat, turtles, crested eagles, and Pryer's woodpeckers, known as noguchigera. A less welcome inhabitant of the area is the extremely poisonous habu snake. It is about two meters long, has a yellow head, and is typically found hiding in thickets or by the sides of roads. It hardly ever goes into cities. If you take precautions, particularly in the spring and fall, you should not experience any issues. If you do get bitten, head to the closest hospital as they should have antivenin.

Get your FREE book

Please visit https://tinyurl.com/travel-with-jeffery for additional resources and to engage with my newsletter.

I also want to reward you for purchasing my book. To get the reward which is a travel planner; kindly click on this link below or open the link on your browser.

https://tinyurl.com/travel-with-jeffery

I hope you love the travel planner!

Brief History of Okinawa

The islands that currently comprise Okinawa were united for the first time in the fifteenth century to form the Ryūkyū kingdom, which was ruled from Shuri Castle in present-day Naha. This is regarded as the golden age of Ryky culture. Trade expanded with China, the remainder of Japan, and other Southeast Asian countries, although the historically non-militarized kingdom retained its independence by paying tribute to China. The Shimazu clan of Kagoshima (southern Kyūshū) then invaded in 1609.

The Ryūkyū rulers became vassals of the Shimazu, who levied severe levies and controlled with an iron fist for the next two centuries, using the islands as a route for trade with China at a time when such interaction was technically prohibited by the Togukawa Shogunate. The islands were simply merged to the mainland as Okinawa Prefecture when the Japanese feudal system was abolished in the 1870s. The Meiji administration constructed a military installation and attempted to eliminate indigenous culture by forcing people to speak Japanese and swear allegiance to the emperor, as well as prohibiting schools from teaching Ryūkyū history.

Okinawa had been pretty successfully assimilated into Japan by the early twentieth century, and it became a critical part in Japan's last line of defense during the Pacific War. Following the battle of Iwō-jima in March 1945, the American fleet advanced on Okinawa and, after an extensive preliminary attack, referred to locally as a "typhoon of steel", the Americans invaded on April 1, 1945. It took nearly three months of fierce battle before the Japanese commander, General Ushijima, committed suicide and the island surrendered. The Battle of Okinawa claimed the lives of 12,500 American troops (plus 37,000 injured) and an estimated 250,000 Japanese civilians, approximately half of whom were locals.

It is estimated that one-third of Okinawa's inhabitants died during the war, many as a result of mass suicides shortly to the surrender, and others as a result of disease and malnutrition. However, rather than America, the islanders' subsequent rage has been focused toward the Japanese government. The majority of people believe Okinawa was sacrificed to defend the mainland - this was the only major conflict fought on Japanese soil - and that they were mislead by Japanese assurances that they were drawing the American fleet into a trap. This was exacerbated by the actions of Japanese troops, who are accused of denying natives shelter and medical assistance before abandoning them to the Americans.

By comparison, the American intruders were a welcome relief, despite the islanders' most severe fears. They brought in much-needed food supplies - Spam was an instant hit in this pork-loving culture, and was a forerunner of the processed luncheon meat seen in pork champur - and gradually helped revive the local economy. Of course, this was not entirely altruistic, as Okinawa was strategically located to monitor events in Southeast Asia. As the Korean War morphed into the Vietnam War in the

1950s, American bases became an indelible part of the Okinawan landscape. Indeed, Okinawa remained under American control until 1972, when local protests resulted in the restoration of Japanese sovereignty.

Since then, the two governments have worked together to keep an American military presence on the island despite growing opposition, which peaked in 1995 when three American servicemen were convicted of raping a 12-year-old schoolgirl.

Okinawa has since witnessed some strange political swings. Local elections in 2007 brought Aiko Shimajiri to power; strangely, his priorities were the local economy rather than military matters. These were to be highlighted in national elections two years later, with Yukio Hatayama elected Prime Minister on a commitment to abolish, rather than relocate, the Futenma air station — his failure to do so saw him resign in disgrace less than a year later.

What is Okinawa most famous for?

If you guessed the Karate Kid, starring Ralph Macchio and Noriyuki "Pat" Morita, you earn a gold star. While Mr. Miyagi's persona is from Okinawa, the majority of the film was shot in Hawaii. Whomp, whomp.

Okinawa, in my opinion, is best known for two things: Okinawa time and the Okinawa diet. Okinawans are believed to having the world's greatest life spans because their traditional food is so abundant in delicious vitamins and nutrients.

Okinawa, in my opinion, is best known for two things: Okinawa time and the Okinawa diet. Okinawans are believed to having the world's greatest life spans because their traditional food is so abundant in delicious vitamins and nutrients.

When I mention Okinawa time... Everything is done gradually and whenever people feel like it. In other words, this nonsense can drive you insane. If I were you, I would avoid public transportation at all costs and instead rent a car while you're in town. Because the reality is, I barely made it six months without a car and spent a fortune on public transportation.

Okinawa is also noted for its beautiful beaches, a blend of Japanese, Chinese, and Korean culture, and its own distinct culture. Okinawa was known as the Ryukyu Kingdom before becoming a part of Japan, and it had its own culture, language, and traditions.

Top tips to know before you go to Okinawa

1. When visiting Okinawa, I would recommend hiring an interpreter and guide because the Okinawans speak their own dialect different from Japanese, and English is not widely spoken among the natives. I recommend that you use this company (oiga.jpn.com/english).
2. They do, however, drive on the same side of the road, so renting a car to explore and travel around is a good option.
3. The main island is only 112 kilometers long and 11 kilometers wide.
4. Try the well-known OTS Rental Cars which has offices at the airport and most hotels and provides cars with English-speaking navigation.
5. Karate was also invented in Okinawa. If this is the reason you're visiting Okinawa, make sure you stop by Dojo bar at least once. It's owned by an Englishman who traveled to Okinawa to

practice karate but fell in love with it so much that he stayed and created a karate-themed pub.

6. The sanshin (three strings) is a musical instrument from Okinawa that predates the Japanese shami-sen.

7. They are a unique and gorgeous instrument that you will see everywhere.

8. If you are interested in war history, particularly World War II history, I recommend spending a day visiting two memorable sites. Begin your day at the former Japanese navy underground headquarters, where in 1944, workers of the Japanese Navy Corps of Engineers excavated a tunnel complex for the navy's Okinawa headquarters bunker. It was opened to the public in 1970 in order to educate future generations about the agony of war and to solicit prayers for long-term world peace.

9. After lunch, visit the Okinawa Prefectural Peace Memorial Museum. This is where the Battle of Okinawa occurred, which claimed the lives of almost 200,000 people. The war wiped out one-

third of the Okinawan people and devastated the island.

10. Visit Tsuboya Pottery Street to learn about the 300-year history of this distinctive Okinawan pottery. They have classes where they teach you how to produce these gorgeous and earthy ceramics that are mostly used for functional purposes rather than just ornamental purposes like its sibling Japanese pottery. The greatest season to visit Okinawa is March/April because of the gentler tropical weather, but you may enjoy scuba diving, fishing, whale watching, and other water sports all year round.

Getting There

With an increase in the number of low-cost airline flights between major Japanese cities and Okinawa, as well as the introduction of new international routes such as Seoul-Okinawa (Jin Air) and Taipei-Okinawa (Peach Aviation), visiting the fascinating island of Okinawa has become easier and more affordable than ever before. Check out the quickest and most cost-effective way to get to Okinawa from your home!

Flights connect Naha Airport with major airports on the mainland, including Tokyo (Haneda, Narita), Osaka (Itami, Kansai), Shizuoka (Fujisan Shizuoka), Ishikawa (Komatsu), Kobe, Nagoya (Centrair), and Fukuoka. Each airline's flight schedule changes by season, with more flights available during the summer months. Transportation from Okinawa's main island to distant islands occurs by plane or ferry. There are also direct flights from the mainland to Ishigaki or Miyako.

Island hopping excursions are highly suggested for individuals who want to experience not only the prime sightseeing locations on Okinawa's main island, but also the outer islands, each with its own attractions. If you want to tour the Yaeyama Islands, Ishigaki Island is a good place to start because it is the key center for inter-island transportation in the area.

With some of the country's leading low-cost airlines, notably Jetstar and Peach Aviation, introducing new routes between Okinawan islands and mainland airports in 2012, visiting Okinawa and its interesting outlying islands has become much easier and more affordable than ever before. The increased number of flights to Ishigaki Island since the inauguration of New Ishigaki Airport has contributed to the growing popularity of Yaeyamas island hopping excursions. Furthermore, in order to compete with low-cost carriers, Japan's major airlines have recently begun offering tickets for the outer islands, such as Ishigaki and Miyako, at lower prices.

Accommodations

Here are the top ten Okinawa hotels and resorts that guarantee more than simply a stay but an unforgettable journey:

1. The Ritz-Carlton, Okinawa:

The Ritz-Carlton, nestled in a tranquil beachfront region, offers a perfect blend of luxury with traditional Okinawan charm. This resort ensures an enjoyable holiday with spacious accommodations overlooking the East China Sea, great service, and a world-class spa.

2. Hilton Okinawa Chatan Resort:

Hilton Okinawa Chatan Resort, which overlooks the lovely Mihama American Village, features a modern design and a variety of services. This hotel caters to both pleasure and business tourists, offering exceptional dining options as well as a private beach.

3. Kafuu Resort Fuchaku Condo Hotel:

Kafuu Resort Fuchaku Condo Hotel is located in the center of Okinawa's resort district and offers a great blend of Okinawan warmth and modern comfort. The ocean-view rooms and numerous eating options make it a popular choice for visitors.

4. Okinawa Marriott Resort & Spa:

Okinawa Marriott Resort & Spa, located on the waterfront, offers a serene vacation with its lush gardens and ocean-facing accommodations. The spa, pool, and numerous restaurants at the resort offer a peaceful visit.

5. Hyatt Regency Seragaki Island, Okinawa:

The Hyatt Regency on Seragaki Island is a must-see for anyone looking for a private retreat. This resort is surrounded by crystal-clear waters and provides magnificent villas, a pristine beach, and a range of aquatic activities.

6. Okinawa EXES Naha:

Okinawa EXES Naha, located in the heart of Naha, blends convenience and luxury. For urban explorers, the hotel's modern style, rooftop pool, and panoramic city views make it a popular choice.

7. Sheraton Okinawa Sunmarina Resort:

Sheraton Okinawa Sunmarina Resort is a family-friendly alternative with a private beach and spectacular views of the East China Sea. The resort offers spacious rooms, a kids' facility, and a variety of eating options.

8. ANA InterContinental Manza Beach Resort:

This ANA InterContinental resort overlooking Manza Beach is the ideal combination of luxury and natural beauty. It is an excellent choice due to its infinity pool, fine restaurants, and proximity to the Okinawa Churaumi Aquarium.

9. Moon Ocean Ginowan Hotel & Residence:

The Moon Ocean Ginowan Hotel & Residence, located along the Ginowan Marina, offers a one-of-a-kind experience with its modern accommodations and stunning views. The hotel's modern architecture and close accessibility to attractions make it a unique option.

10. Naha Terrace:

Naha Terrace is an urban refuge for people looking for a taste of Okinawa's capital. This hotel caters to discerning tourists with a refined setting, fine dining options, and a convenient location.

Okinawa's numerous hotel offers ensure that there is something for every guest, whether they are searching for a seaside vacation, a cultural immersion, or a city escape. Book your stay intelligently and allow the beauty of Okinawa to emerge in front of you.

Transportation

Renting a Car

Because of competition among rival companies, rental car fees in Okinawa, as in the rest of Japan, are comparatively low. Average daily prices begin at 2,000 yen for a light car (with a 550-cc engine or less), 2,500 yen for a tiny 1,000 cc van, and 5,000 yen for a van seating six or more passengers.

Because of competition among rival companies, rental car fees in Okinawa, as in the rest of Japan, are comparatively low. Average daily prices begin at 2,000 yen for a light car (with a 550-cc engine or less), 2,500 yen for a tiny 1,000 cc van, and 5,000 yen for a van seating six or more passengers. However, not all rental car companies offer support in foreign languages, so it is better to find one that does. The majority of automobile rental firms are located near Naha Airport and at T Galleria Okinawa by DFS in Shintoshin, with some having branch offices in the resort hotel towns of Chatan and Onna Village, where you can pick up your rental car.

Multilingual navigation systems in Korean, Japanese, English, and Chinese are being installed by some automobile rental companies. Car rental firms provide free airport pick-up and drop-off, but a popular alternative is to take the monorail directly from the airport to Omoromachi Station (about 19 minutes) and hire a car at the nearby hire-a-Car Depot (in T Galleria Okinawa by DFS).

Make cautious to confirm what is included in the price before you arrive, because even if the basic rate is modest, the complete amount might become rather pricey after insurance payments are included. Furthermore, making a reservation ahead of time is strongly advised, especially during busy months such as Japanese holidays, Golden Week (end of April to beginning of May), Obon (mid-August), and autumn. Examine numerous options because a hotel or rental car package through a travel agency is sometimes less expensive.

To hire a car, an international driving permit or a driver's license issued in Switzerland, Germany, France, Belgium, Slovenia, Monaco, or Taiwan must be presented, along with a translation from the applicable embassy or consulate in Japan or the Japan Automobile Federation (JAF).

Car rental companies offering services in English

Rental	Number
Budget Car Rental	098-857-1813
Fuji Rent-a-Car	098-858-9330
Times Car Rental	098-860-7272
Toyota Rent-a-Car	098-857-0100
Nippon Rent-a-Car	098-859-0919
OTS Rent-a-Car	098-860-7700
ABC Rent-a-Car	098-916-8593

Bus

With no rail or subway service, vehicles, buses, taxis, and vehicle charter services are the principal modes of transportation on Okinawa. When commuting within Naha's downtown region, the Yui Rail, a monorail system that runs across the city, is a convenient mode of transportation. Bus rates differ depending on the route, company, and type of bus used. Passengers on ordinary local buses must pay the exact fare in yen cash (bill and coin changers are available on board).

In some instances, the city line bus stop is located separately from the suburban line bus stop. Keep in mind that, while arrival times are indicated at bus stations, they are not always reliable because they fluctuate owing to traffic. Make sure you get on the appropriate bus, especially on Kokusai Street, where there are multiple busses. To avoid the danger of the driver missing you at the stop, notify your presence by raising your hand.

Fill the fare box with only the exact amount of fare. Bills (only 1,000 yen bills) should be changed with the bill changer. The coin changer accepts 500 yen, 100 yen, and 50 yen coins. However, on city route buses and select suburban routes, you will automatically receive change.

In a traffic gridlock, be wary of empty lanes. Okinawa is a society that relies heavily on private vehicles as its major mode of transportation. Because of this, key highways on the island are extremely congested during the morning and evening rush hours on weekdays. To alleviate traffic congestion, some lanes are allocated to buses, excluding most other vehicles; nevertheless, taxis, motorbikes, and specially exempted vehicles are permitted in bus lanes in addition to buses. Police officers conduct random checks and issue tickets with fines ranging from 6,000 to 7,000 yen to motorists who violate bus lane guidelines.

The Okinawa Expressway is a 57.3-kilometer toll road that connects Nago in the north to Naha in the south. While Highway 58 takes nearly two hours to drive between those locations, the expressway takes roughly one hour. Motorists on the expressway must adhere to the 80 km/h speed restriction at all times. The Naha Airport Road (no toll) connects the Nishihara I.C. near the US Consulate General in Urasoe City to the Nakachi I.C., about 10 minutes from Naha Airport.

Furthermore, the Yaka I.C. entrance only allows travel in the direction of Naha, whereas the Kishaba I.C. entrance is restricted to minicars and ordinary vehicles registered in the electric toll collection (ETC) system and, once again, only allows travel in the direction of Naha, and is open between 6:00 and 22:00. To pay the toll, present your ticket to the attendant as you exit the highway and pay the fee displayed on the screen to the right of your vehicle. To use the ETC, you must install a particular device on your vehicle, which can be obtained at auto accessories stores, and register in the system.

Okinawa Urban Monorail

The monorail is the finest way to go about Naha City. During the summer tourism season, traffic becomes more congested, and parking is quite expensive. Due to severe traffic, it takes 60 minutes or more to drive from Naha Airport to Shuri; however, the monorail runs 12.9 kilometers (about 8 miles) in 27 minutes from Naha Airport to Shuri, allowing you to cut a bus or taxi ride by 15 to 42 minutes. After the monorail began operations, new shopping complexes and stores were developed around each station.

The new Okinawa Prefectural Museum, which opened in November 2007, as well as T Galleria Okinawa by DFS and huge shopping centers, are located in the Shintoshin region around Omoromachi Station. On a clear day, you may be able to see the Kerama Islands from Yui Rail, which is 20 meters (66 feet) above the ground. The Shuri district is 1,000 meters (0.621 miles) above sea level and offers views of Urasoe City, which is adjacent to Naha City.

Taxi

Cars and buses are the principal modes of transportation on Okinawa, with the exception of the monorail, which operates primarily within Naha City. Many bus services, including route maps, are, however, not available in English. Local bus operations might be complex for first-time customers who are unfamiliar with the system or the area. It is not a viable alternative for individuals with a restricted amount of time to spend on the island. To get around on their own, many tourists utilize cabs or rent cars.

Language Tips

Basic Phrases

Let's delve into some basic phrases that can enhance the experience for travelers in Okinawa:

"Hello! How are you?" *(Haisai! Shima senka?)*

"Thank you very much!" *(Nifee deebiru ganun!)*

"Excuse me, where is the beach?"

(Shima kataa beachu ikkona?)

"I would like Okinawa soba, please." *(Uchinaa soba chuunnaa)*

This place is beautiful!" *(Koko yasaa ko yabai ne!)*

"Goodbye! See you later!" *(Sayonara! Yoi sho-i!)*

"How much does this cost?" *(Kuchaguachu ikkona?)*

"Help! Call the police!" *(Tasuketee! Porisu Uchinaa manchuukoo!)*

Remember, Okinawa has a distinct culture and language, so using some basic phrases in the local dialect can not only facilitate communication but also show respect for the island's unique identity.

Language Apps

These apps are not only user-friendly, but they are also adapted to the unique characteristics of the Okinawan region.

Using Google Translate:

Google Translate, while not particular to Okinawa, is a robust tool that handles several languages, including Japanese. Its real-time translation feature, which uses your phone's camera, can be very useful for reading signs or menus. Remember that Okinawa has its own distinct dialect, so knowing a few popular words will come in handy.

Learn Okinawan Phrases:

Consider using apps like "Learn Okinawan Phrases" to learn more about the local culture. These apps provide curated selections of key phrases and idioms in both standard Japanese and Okinawan. This is especially useful when communicating with locals who may prefer to communicate in their own language.

HelloTalk:

HelloTalk connects you with native speakers for language exchange for a more dynamic learning experience. This software allows you to practice your Japanese or Okinawan with native speakers who are also learning your language. It's a great opportunity to meet new people and learn about Okinawa's best kept secrets.

Tandem:

Tandem, like HelloTalk, links language learners all around the world. Conversations with native Japanese speakers or with travelers planning their Okinawan vacation are recommended. This app allows you to improve your language abilities while connecting with others who share your interest in exploring.

Okinawa Travel Guide Apps:

Consider Okinawa travel guide applications, which frequently offer language portions. Apps like "Okinawa Travel Guide" and "Okinawa Offline Map" give travelers with vital insights about local customs, traditions, and essential terminology. These manuals are frequently available offline, ensuring accessible even in remote regions.

iTranslate:

iTranslate is a useful tool that supports Japanese and may be used for quick translations on the fly. Its voice recognition technology allows you to speak phrases directly into your tablet for immediate translation, removing any potential language obstacles.

Jisho (Japanese Dictionary):

Having a Japanese-English dictionary app on your phone, such as Jisho, can be extremely beneficial. It includes extensive explanations of terms and phrases, allowing you to understand the nuances of the language and easily navigate conversations.

While these language programs are useful, immersing yourself in local culture is the key to having a truly enriching stay in Okinawa. Don't be afraid to move outside your comfort zone, practice your new words, and enjoy the warm welcome of the Okinawan people.

What to Pack to Okinawa

I'm going to go out on a limb here and say you're going to Okinawa in the summer. One thing I noticed is that Japan is very strict with baggage restrictions and regulations. So, if you are from USA... This is terrible news for you. I personally like the American Tourister suitcase. It's tough, durable and you can beat it and it's still intact.

Also, the dimensions of 22" x 15" x 9.5" are perfect for luggage and you don't have to check your luggage. I also recommend getting the Bagail luggage cubes to stay organized and fit as much as possible into a small space. If your luggage is safely stored at your accommodation, it is best to use a beach bag or backpack. I recommend the Fjall Raven backpack because it's really good anti-theft (not that you need to worry because crime is so low in Japan) and you can safely carry essentials like your laptop and camera.

Things to Do in Okinawa

1. Take a Hike

Despite having some of Japan's best beaches, many activities to do in Okinawa have nothing to do with water. Okinawa, in particular, is a hiking paradise. Some of my favorite climbs on the main island are the relatively short ones up to the ruins of Nakijin Castle or up to the keep of Shuri Castle near Naha city.

Mount Gusuku on Ie provides breathtaking views, while Mt. Omoto on Ishigaki combines breathtaking panoramas with crystalline waterfalls.

2. Go Under the Sea (or Boat on Top of It)

Okinawa diving is among of the best in Asia (and virtually by default, the best in Japan), although it can be pricier than you've found elsewhere. Okinawa's top diving spots include the Kerama Islands, which are located immediately off the main island, as well as the Yaeyama region, which contains Ishigaki. Note that diving licenses are strictly enforced in Japan; if you don't have one when you arrive in Okinawa, your only choice will be to snorkel. Renting a canoe or kayak is another option to experience Okinawa's gorgeous sea.

3. Hit the Beach (or at Least Look At It)

What's the bad news? Even compiling a short list of Okinawa's top beaches can be challenging, especially if you have the time and desire to go island-hopping. What's the good news? If you're looking for a quick getaway in Okinawa, consider Ishigaki's Kabira Bay and Aharen Beach on Tokashiki island (just north of the main island). It should be noted that in the case of Kabira Bay, which is protected, you will not be permitted to enter the sea (but you will be able to take some amazing photos!).

4. Sticking to the City

All of this is not to mean that you must wear hiking boots or a swimsuit to enjoy Okinawa touring. In truth, there's plenty to see and do in Naha, from the aforementioned Shuri Castle to the tranquil Shikina-en park and the enigmatic Naminoue Shrine, which rises above the city. Naha also has the Okinawa Prefectural Museum & Art Museum, where you may study about the once-sovereign Kingdom of Ryukyu, which ruled over Okinawa before being absorbed by the Japanese Empire.

5. Check Out Kokusai-dori

Kokusai-dori, a 1.6-kilometer-long street in the city center, is one of Okinawa's most renowned streets. Many tourists and residents converge here, and it is frequently a site where markets, cuisine, and entertainment are intermingled.

Many visitors believe there are wonderful souvenir selections to bring home from Japan, so if you need a last-minute gift, head to Kokusai-dori. People can wander around and shop on the street throughout the week, just like any other public street, with shops and companies shutting at certain times.

Kouri Bridge View Point

If you're looking for stunning views of the lake and city, I will recommend you to pay a visit to Kouri Bridge View Point. People can visit the longest toll-free bridge in Japan, which spans more than one mile, as well as the surrounding nature regions.

Much of Okinawa is green and scenic, and this bridge magnifies that. The Kouri Bridge View Point allows pedestrians to enjoy the city's surroundings while being projected in the sky. It's also worth noting that this bridge connects two islands, making it a necessary mode of transportation for many locals.

Address: Sumuide, Nago, Okinawa 905-1635, Japan

Hours of operation: 24 hours a day, 7 days a week

6. Stroll Through Peace Memorial Park

One thing to do in Okinawa, Japan, is walk around the Peace Memorial Park, a community place devoted to nearly a third of their population who died in WW2 as a result of both sides' actions. Many people find this memorial park to be quite peaceful, and it's a good place to pay homage to those who died during the conflict.

This park was constructed by the city to bring hope and calm to individuals who have been affected by violence and heartbreak, making it a standout destination on our list. One thing to keep in mind is that visitors are advised to keep quiet and not make too much of a fuss while they are here. Although it is a park, it must also be treated as a memorial.

7. Buy Goods at The Makishi Public Market

The Makishi Public Market, which houses Naha's principal produce, meat, seafood, and general retail market, is the next thing to do in Okinawa, Japan. Throughout the week, guests can find food and other products for sale at an indoor marketplace.

For many, the seafood stands out because it is fished fresh and served directly to clients by Makishi sellers. It's similar to what we'd call a farmer's market in the West, and it's a great opportunity to support local companies.

8. Visit Shuri Castle

Okinawa was an independent kingdom known as the Ryukyu Kingdom before becoming a Japanese prefecture in 1879. As a result, the island's culture and history are distinct from the rest of the country.

Shuri Castle was the royal palace throughout the kingdom's reign and has a special place in Okinawan history and culture. Despite being completely destroyed during WWII, it was reconstructed in the 1990s and designated a UNESCO World Heritage Site.

Today, it attracts thousands of tourists and is one of Okinawa's most visited landmarks.

9. Have Fun at Okinawa World

Okinawa World is a theme park in the southern part of the main island that offers a variety of exciting activities to visitors. There is much to keep people entertained, from glassblowing and craft creation to drum performances.

The 850-meter Gyokusendo cave, however, is the highlight of Okinawa World. It contains a beautiful succession of stalactites and stalagmites that will astound visitors.

Outside the cave, guests can browse the various local vendors for cute Japanese items. The site also contains a snake museum where visitors may watch snake shows and learn about the deadly Habu snake.

10. Explore The Mihama Americana Village

Mihama Americana Village on Okinawa is a slice of America in Japan. The village, inspired by Seaport Village in San Diego, is a big shopping area with a unique mix of stores built atop a former US airfield.

It exudes West Coast characteristics and will be the ideal playground for homesick American travelers, with restaurants, cafés, shops, and retail stores as well as karaoke studios. The American-themed enterprise has a massive Ferris wheel and a popular movie theater. It's also an excellent location for watching the sunset over the beach.

Must-Visit Destinations

Naha

Welcome to Naha, Okinawa's bustling capital, where old traditions coexist with modern metropolitan life. Naha, located in the island's south, serves as the gateway to Okinawa's distinct cultural heritage, scenic beaches, and wonderful cuisine. We'll delve into the heart of Naha in this travel guide, unearthing its hidden gems and offering you with a unique experience that goes beyond the conventional tourist track.

Naha has a rich history, which is reflected in its well-preserved landmarks. Begin your adventure at Shuri Castle, a UNESCO World Heritage Site and historic Ryukyu Kingdom palace. It is a striking sight because to its brilliant red hue and complex architectural elements. As you explore the castle grounds, you'll learn about the island's royal history and its impact on Okinawan culture.

Shikina-en Garden, a tranquil refuge adjacent to Shuri Castle, was originally the Ryukyu royal family's second residence. Stroll around the gardens, which feature traditional Okinawan vegetation, exquisite bridges, and quiet ponds. It's a tranquil haven that offers a look of the island's aristocratic lifestyle.

To completely immerse yourself in the local culture, visit Naha's lively shopping and entertainment center, Kokusai Street. Kokusai Street, which is lined with shops, boutiques, and cafes, is the ideal place to experience Okinawan delicacies like Rafute (braised pork belly) and try traditional crafts. Don't pass up the chance to purchase one-of-a-kind souvenirs, such as locally crafted pottery and vivid textiles.

Visit the Tamaudun Mausoleum, the ultimate resting place of the Ryukyu monarchs, to gain a better knowledge of Okinawa's spiritual practices. The hallowed ambiance and old objects of the mausoleum provide insight into the island's spiritual traditions.

Naha is not only a cultural center; it is also a gateway to Okinawa's breathtaking natural beauty. Take a short ferry ride to the adjacent Kerama Islands, which are known for their clean waters and vibrant coral reefs. Snorkeling and diving aficionados will be amazed by the variety of marine life, which includes bright tropical fish and stately sea turtles.

Back on the main island, don't miss the Okinawa Peace Memorial Park, which is devoted to the victims of World War II's Battle of Okinawa. The park's beautiful surrounds and moving memorials provide a tranquil setting for introspection and memory.

A trip to Naha isn't complete unless you try the local cuisine. Enjoy Okinawa's distinct food culture, which combines elements from Japan, China, and Southeast Asia. Try the famous Okinawa soba, a noodle dish served in a savory broth, or the Goya Champuru, a stir-fry with the island's unique ingredients.

As the day comes to an end, visit Naha's izakayas (Japanese bars) and sip awamori, the island's native distilled alcohol. Conversation with locals will most likely reveal the warmth and hospitality that define Okinawan culture.

Shuri Castle

Shuri Castle, a UNESCO World Heritage Site, is a tribute to the Ryukyuan people's tenacity and architectural brilliance. The castle was built in the 14th century and has undergone numerous restorations and repairs, each layer contributing to its particular appeal. The architecture's brilliant reds and detailed embellishments reflect the particular blend of Okinawan, Chinese, and Japanese influences.

When tourists enter the castle grounds, they are transported to the Ryukyu Kingdom era. The finely planted gardens, filled with traditional Shisa lion statues and bright flora, create a tranquil setting for the historical voyage. Exploring the castle's many courtyards and features, such as the Seiden (main hall) and the Shureimon gate, provides an insight into the richness and elegance of the Ryukyuan royal court.

The stories that resonate within the castle's walls cannot not but enthrall. For centuries, Shuri Castle functioned as the Ryukyu Kingdom's political and administrative center, influencing the destiny of the islands and cultivating a distinct cultural identity. With its magnificent throne room and delicate wooden partitions, the Seiden bears silent testimony to the festivities and rituals that previously took place within its walls.

The historical relevance of the castle extends beyond its role as a seat of sovereignty. It was critical in encouraging cultural interchange between Okinawa and other areas. The fusion of architectural forms and the use of meticulous craftsmanship in the interiors demonstrate Okinawa's cultural syncretism. The castle includes interactive exhibits and displays that provide insights into the Ryukyuan people's daily lives to enhance the visiting experience. Shuri Castle's museum highlights the concrete and intangible parts of Okinawa's legacy, encouraging a deeper understanding for the island's unique cultural tapestry.

The place takes on a lovely aura when the sun sets over Shuri Castle, putting a warm glow on its aged walls. Evening illuminations enhance the splendor of the castle, producing a mesmerizing scene that inspires study and thought.

A visit to Shuri Castle is more than just a voyage through time; it is an immersion into Okinawa's essence. The castle is a symbol of the Ryukyuan people's endurance, cultural diversity, and perseverance. Shuri Castle welcomes you with open arms, guaranteeing a memorable experience in the heart of Okinawa's capital, whether you are a history enthusiast, a cultural adventurer, or simply someone seeking the enchantment of a bygone period.

Kokusai Street

Kokusai Street is a cultural crossroads as well as a shopping and dining destination. Street entertainers and musicians frequently contribute to the excitement by delivering unexpected entertainment that captivates passerby. Participate in a traditional dance or the lively beats of a street-side taiko drum performance if you interact with the locals.

Explore the tucked-away side lanes that offer hidden gems for a respite from the vibrant energy of Kokusai Street. Serene cafes, art galleries, and tiny parks provide a more tranquil respite, allowing you to see Naha's softer side.

Naha's Kokusai Street is more than simply a street; it's a sensory trip through Okinawa's past and present. Kokusai Street encompasses the essence of Okinawa's personality, making it a must-visit location for anybody seeking a genuine and engaging travel experience, whether you're relishing local flavors, discovering unusual boutiques, or immersing yourself in the active street culture.

Northern Okinawa

When visiting the northern section of Okinawa, two gems stand out among the many attractions, each offering a distinct combination of natural marvels and cultural depth.

Cape Hedo

If you travel to Okinawa's northernmost tip, you will come upon the breathtaking Cape Hedo. The panoramic vista of the wide blue ocean meeting the rough rocks is nothing short of amazing as the Pacific Ocean breezes embrace you. It's a moment when the earth and sky seem to merge, and you become one with nature.

The journey to Cape Hedo is an adventure in and of itself, with gorgeous paths taking you past lush subtropical forests and charming settlements. Once there, take a leisurely stroll along the well-kept pathways, allowing the fresh sea wind to energise your senses. The Cape Hedo Observation Tower stands majestically, offering an unrivaled vantage point from which to take in the grandeur that spreads as far as the eye can see.

Don't forget to bring your camera! The breathtaking cliffs, deep blue sea, and colorful foliage create for postcard-worthy photographs. Cape Hedo is more than a destination; it's a meeting with nature's magnificence.

Okinawa Churaumi Aquarium

Visit the Okinawa Churaumi Aquarium for a different but equally enchanting experience. This world-class aquarium, located at Ocean Expo Park, invites you to explore the enthralling depths of the Pacific Ocean. It's more than simply an aquarium; it's a journey into the underwater treasures that survive.

The Kuroshio Tank, the major attraction, is one of the largest of its kind, containing beautiful whale sharks and a diverse array of marine life. As you stand in front of the big acrylic window, it's as if you've been transported to another universe where the ocean's giants float by gracefully.

The Dolphin Lagoon provides a more engaging experience, allowing you to watch dolphin intellect and agility in exciting shows. The touch pools allow visitors to interact with smaller aquatic species, making it a fascinating and instructive experience for all ages.

The Okinawa Churaumi Aquarium, surrounded by beautiful foliage and the soothing tones of the water, is more than just an attraction; it's a complete experience that honors the richness of Okinawa's marine heritage.

Cape Hedo and the Okinawa Churaumi Aquarium weave a tapestry of experiences that display the island's various beauty in Okinawa's northern reaches. Whether you're drawn to the wild grandeur of nature at Cape Hedo or the enthralling undersea world at the aquarium, each destination guarantees an out-of-the-ordinary trip.

As you embark on your Okinawan adventure, allow the northern wonders to make an unforgettable stamp on your travel book, reminding you that some experiences are best articulated through the whispering of the wind and the dance of the ocean's depths.

Ishigaki

Ishigaki is a treasure trove of natural beauty and cultural riches, providing an out-of-the-ordinary experience. If you're planning a trip to Okinawa, don't forget to stop at Kabira Bay and Iriomote Island on the island of Ishigaki.

Kabira Bay

Kabira Bay, with its crystalline seas and scenic sceneries, is a jewel in the crown of Ishigaki. The bay is well-known for its vibrant coral reefs and marine life, making it a snorkeling and diving paradise. The turquoise waters, flanked by white sand beaches and lush flora, make for a picture-perfect environment.

Consider taking a glass-bottom boat excursion to really immerse yourself in the magnificence of

Kabira Bay. Glide through the azure water, taking in the kaleidoscope of aquatic life underneath you. The bay is also home to rare black pearls, and you can learn about the traditional art of pearl cultivation at the local pearl farms.

Don't forget to sample the local fare at the seafood eateries that line the bay. Freshly fished delicacies like Ishigaki beef and Okinawan specialties provide a gourmet trip that compliments the breathtaking surroundings.

Iriomote Island

Iriomote Island, just a ferry ride from Ishigaki, entices with its lush jungles, mangrove forests, and wild beauty. This island, known as the "Galapagos of the East," is a refuge for nature lovers. The lovely Urauchi River, Okinawa's longest river, is one of the attractions, flanked by deep mangrove woods.

Set off on a kayak excursion down the Urauchi River to see the mangrove ecology and the numerous bird species that live there. Hiking trails lead to the awe-inspiring Pinaisara Falls, a beautiful cascade surrounded by verdant landscapes, for the more daring.

Water sports on Iriomote Island include snorkeling and paddleboarding in the crystal-clear waters of the Nakama River. Keep a watch out for the elusive Iriomote wildcat, a unique species native to the region, as you explore the island.

Ishigaki, with its enchanting Kabira Bay and natural beauties of Iriomote Island, invites you to discover Okinawa's soul. In this lovely corner of Japan, immerse yourself in the vivid marine life, indulge in local cuisines, and connect with nature. Ishigaki is a trip into the core of Okinawa's beauty and culture, not merely a destination.

Get your FREE book

Please visit https://tinyurl.com/travel-with-jeffery for additional resources and to engage with my newsletter.

I also want to reward you for purchasing my book. To get the reward which is a travel planner; kindly click on this link below or open the link on your browser.

https://tinyurl.com/travel-with-jeffery

I hope you love the travel planner!

Miyako

Sunayama Beach in Miyako and the picturesque Ikema Island stand out as highlights of this paradisiacal location. Let us delve into the charm of these locations and discover the hidden riches that await the adventurous tourist.

Sunayama Beach

Sunayama Beach, located in the center of Miyako, is a magnificent expanse of golden sands bordered by crystal-clear azure waters. Its name, "Sunayama," translates to "sand mountain," a reference to the dunes that line the shoreline. A sense of tranquility envelops the beach as the gentle waves caress the sand, making it an ideal site for rest and introspection.

Aside from its peaceful atmosphere, Sunayama Beach has a variety of activities to suit any traveler's preferences. Exploring the colorful marine life that flourishes beneath the surface is possible through thrilling water sports such as snorkeling and kayaking. A sunset stroll down the shore is a must for anyone looking for a more leisurely experience, as the sun paints the sky in orange and pink hues, spreading a warm glow over the area.

No trip is complete unless you try the local cuisine. Along the shore, small kiosks sell Okinawan specialties ranging from savory taco rice to refreshing shikuwasa drink. Engage with the friendly residents and you may discover the best-kept culinary secrets of Sunayama.

Ikema Island

Ikema Island, just a short distance from Miyako, appears as a secret gem awaiting discovery. The island, which is connected to Miyako by the historic Ikema Ohashi Bridge, is a refuge of natural beauty and cultural richness.

Ikema Island is a sanctuary for nature lovers, with well-kept trails winding through lush landscapes and offering spectacular panoramic vistas. Whether you want to trek or cycle, the island's paths guarantee an immersive experience that will allow you to connect with Okinawa's natural beauty.

Visit local villages and interact with the friendly locals to immerse yourself in the island's culture. Experience traditional Ryukyuan dance performances and savor the distinct flavors of Ikema's Okinawan cuisine.

The historic Ikema Ohashi Bridge not only connects Miyako and Ikema but also offers breathtaking views. The panoramic views of the East China Sea and neighboring islands emerge as you cross the bridge, producing a visual spectacle that captures the essence of Okinawa's natural grandeur.

Sunayama Beach in Miyako and Ikema Island call with their distinct attractions in the heart of Okinawa. These sites provide an authentic and enriching experience, whether you want calm on the sandy coastlines or adventure along the island paths. Discover the secrets of Sunayama Beach and Ikema Island, and watch Okinawa's enchantment blossom before your eyes.

Traditional Okinawan Arts

Eisa Dance

Eisa is a lively performance art that combines rhythmic beats, vivid costumes, and the community's combined energy. As you travel around Okinawa, don't miss out on the charm of Eisa, a dance form that not only entertains but also recounts the tale of the island's perseverance and spirit.

Eisa Dance originated during the Obon festival, when Okinawan towns gathered to honor their ancestors. The dance is a celebration of life, a rhythmic tribute that connects with Okinawa's throbbing heart. The frenetic drumming, joined by the resonant spin of taiko drums, produces an addictive mood that draws in both locals and visitors.

Under a starlit Okinawan sky, performers dressed in vivid costumes move in time to the throbbing rhythm. The dance is a vivid display of joy, unity, and the people's indomitable spirit. Traditional instruments like as the sanshin give a melodic element to the performance, taking viewers to a realm where time appears to be suspended.

Attend one of the many Eisa festivals to properly understand the core of this cultural treasure. The Eisa Festival in Naha, celebrated every year, is a sight not to be missed. Local troupes, each with its own distinct style, join forces to create a kaleidoscope of colors and sounds. You'll get swept up in the infectious enthusiasm as you watch, and you might even be persuaded to join the dancers and become a part of the living, breathing tradition.

Eisa Dance connects the past and the present, demonstrating Okinawa's enduring legacy. Take the opportunity to interact with residents who are ready to tell the history behind this beautiful dance as you explore the island. You might find yourself learning the fundamentals or hearing anecdotes that lend depth to the performance.

Okinawa gives its heart to anyone who are prepared to listen to the rhythm of Eisa. So, whether you're a history buff, an arts enthusiast, or simply someone wishing to experience a place's soul, Eisa Dance invites you to join in the celebration and become a part of Okinawa's living tale.

Sanshin Music

Sanshin music reflects the islands' rich cultural past. Sanshin, also known as the Okinawan shamisen, is a traditional three-stringed instrument with a particular sound that encapsulates Okinawan history and culture. It is an important component of Okinawan performing arts and has profound cultural roots.

Sanshin has a long and illustrious history that may be traced back to the Chinese sanxian. The instrument arrived in Okinawa years ago and evolved into the distinctive Sanshin we know today. Sanshin, which was formerly linked with Okinawan royalty, progressively became more available to the general population, becoming a vital component of everyday life and celebrations.

Sanshin music is distinguished by its passionate and expressive qualities. The instrument is frequently used to accompany traditional Okinawan melodies that convey stories about love, nature, and the island's history. The tunes are hauntingly beautiful, representing Okinawan culture's unique blend of influences from China, Japan, and Southeast Asia over the years.

Visitors to Okinawa can hear the lovely sounds of Sanshin music at numerous performances and festivals throughout the islands. Local players, sometimes dressed in vibrant traditional garb, expertly play the Sanshin, enthralling audiences with both the sound and the instrument's unusual appearance.

Okinawa provides possibilities for anyone interested in the magic of Sanshin to dive deeper into the art. Visitors can attend workshops and classes where professional instructors will teach them the methods and intricacies of playing the Sanshin. This hands-on encounter instills a deep respect for the devotion and expertise required to learn this classic instrument.

There has been a concentrated effort in recent years to conserve and promote Sanshin music. Individuals and organizations are working hard to guarantee that this important component of Okinawan culture is passed along to future generations. Sanshin's continuous popularity attests to its enduring significance in Okinawa's cultural landscape.

While visiting Okinawa, make sure to immerse yourself in the wonderful world of Sanshin music. Sanshin is a cultural treasure that adds a melodious layer to the vivid tapestry of Okinawa's past, whether it's a live performance at a local festival or the opportunity to try your hand at playing this distinctive instrument.

Culinary Delights

Okinawan Cuisine

The emphasis on fresh, locally obtained ingredients is one of Okinawan cuisine's distinguishing qualities. Because of the subtropical environment, the islands have a plethora of fruits and vegetables, which contributes to the uniqueness of the dishes. Many traditional Okinawan cuisines feature items native to the island, such as sweet potatoes, goya (bitter melon), and the legendary Okinawan purple yam, popularly known as beni-imo.

When it comes to proteins, Okinawa has its own distinct selection. Rafute, or braised pork belly, is a must-try for meat lovers. Slow-cooked pork is infused with a delightful blend of sweet and savory tastes. Goya Champuru, a stir-fry meal with goya, tofu, pork, and other fresh veggies, is another local favorite. The bitter taste of goya gives the dish a distinct edge, giving it a true depiction of Okinawan culinary creativity.

Okinawa is also a heaven for seafood lovers. Because of their coastal location, the islands provide a variety of fresh and tasty marine pleasures. Okinawa Soba is a classic Okinawan cuisine with a savory broth loaded with tender pork belly, green onions, and red pickled ginger served over a bed of thick wheat noodles. It's a hearty dish that encapsulates the spirit of Okinawa's culinary identity.

Don't pass up the opportunity to visit the local markets and street food vendors that highlight the variety of Okinawan foods. The street food scene offers a pleasant voyage for your taste buds, from exquisite taco rice, a blend of Tex-Mex and Okinawan flavors, to the legendary beni-imo tart, a sweet dessert created from the purple yam.

Attending a traditional Okinawan dine known as "kaiseki" is a requirement for those wishing to experience the cultural side of Okinawan cuisine. These multi-course feasts highlight the culinary prowess of the island by providing a carefully picked variety of delicacies.

Okinawan cuisine honors regional flavors, seasonal ingredients, and a rich cultural legacy. Exploring the broad range of meals, from hearty pork-based stews to fresh and savory seafood offerings, is an essential element of any Okinawa Islands visit. Savor the flavors, immerse yourself in the local food culture, and enjoy the unique blend of tradition and innovation that defines Okinawan cuisine as you embark on your gastronomic tour.

Popular Local Dishes

From spicy to sweet, Okinawa's cuisine is a balanced blend of history and innovation, highlighting the region's distinct characteristics.

- **Goya Champuru**

The renowned Goya Champuru, a stir-fry masterpiece, kicks off your Okinawan culinary adventure. Along with tofu, pork, and other fresh ingredients, goya, a slightly bitter indigenous vegetable, takes center stage. As a result, the dish not only entices your taste buds but also captures the essence of Okinawan home cooking.

- **Rafute**

Rafute is a must-try for those looking for a melt-in-your-mouth delight. Pork belly braised to perfection in soy, sake, and mirin in this slow-cooked recipe. The finished result is a soft, delicious delicacy that exemplifies Okinawa's skill in transforming simple ingredients into gourmet marvels.

- **Okinawa Soba**

No trip to Okinawa is complete without trying Okinawa Soba. Buckwheat noodles are the star of the show, supported by a flavorful broth and topped with green onions, scarlet pickled ginger, and tender pork belly. It's a filling dish that captures the island's distinct culinary identity.

- **Beni-imo Tarts**

Beni-imo Tarts, a delectable Okinawan dish, will satisfy your sweet taste. Purple sweet potatoes, known as beni-imo in the Philippines, are converted into a velvety filling covered in a buttery tart shell. As a result, a sweet delicacy that perfectly mixes tradition with a modern twist has been created.

- **Taco Rice**

Taco Rice, a dish that mixes aspects of Tex-Mex and Japanese cuisine, represents Okinawa's culinary fusion. A flavorful medley of ground pork, cheese, lettuce, and tomatoes sits above a bed of rice, creating a flavorful medley that exemplifies Okinawa's receptivity to many influences.

Every food in Okinawa has a story, and every taste is a trip through the island's unique history and culture. Okinawa's culinary landscape is a monument to its people's innovation and enthusiasm, from the umami-rich Goya Champuru to the sweet delight of Beni-imo Tarts. While exploring the island's stunning surroundings and immersing yourself in its unique traditions, make sure to treat your palate to the vast and delectable assortment of native foods that the island has to offer.

Popular Restaurant to dine in Okinawa

Okinawa has a diverse range of food alternatives. Let's have a look at some prominent eateries that promise a memorable gastronomic experience.

- **Nakayukui Market:**

Nakayukui Market is the place to go for a real taste of Okinawan cuisine. This busy market in Naha is a treasure trove of regional cuisines. From fresh seafood and tropical fruits to traditional snacks, Nakayukui Market lets you experience Okinawa's rich hues and sensations. For a true taste of the island, try the famed Okinawan doughnuts, "beni-imo tarts," and Agu pig dishes.

- **Ryukyu Kebab (Japanese Kebab):**

Ryukyu Kebab in Chatan offers a delectable blend of Okinawan and Middle Eastern flavors for a one-of-a-kind fusion experience. The pleasant environment and the aroma of grilling skewers welcome you as you eat dishes like Ishigaki beef kebabs and shawarma wraps made with fresh ingredients from the region. The varied menu appeals to all tastes, making it the ideal location for a relaxed yet flavorful dining experience.

- **Shabu-Shabu Onyasai:**

Shabu-Shabu Onyasai offers an interactive shabu-shabu dining experience. This restaurant, which has many locations throughout Okinawa, allows you to prepare your own thinly sliced meat, fresh vegetables, and noodles in a seething hot pot. The high quality of the food and the communal nature of the dinner make it an excellent choice for those seeking a traditional Japanese dining experience.

- **Hirugi:**

Hirugi in Itoman City is a hidden treasure for fish lovers. This restaurant, which overlooks the beautiful seaside, specializes in fresh catch-of-the-day seafood served with a modern touch. Every dish, from sashimi platters to grilled seafood, exemplifies Okinawa's coastal culinary brilliance. The serene ambiance lends a sense of calm to your dining experience.

- **Makishi Public Market:**

Makishi Public Market, located in the heart of Naha, is a busy gathering place for locals and tourists to explore Okinawa's culinary diversity. The market is packed with food kiosks selling everything from sushi and tempura to Okinawan soba. Take a seat at one of the community tables, soak up the lively environment, and let your taste buds explore the plethora of tastes on offer.

Okinawa's culinary sector is as diverse as its terrain, combining tradition and innovation. Okinawa's restaurants promise a journey of pleasures that will linger in your memory long after your vacation, whether you're exploring local markets, eating fusion meals, or enjoying the simplicity of a hot pot. Set out to discover these popular dining venues, and let Okinawa's flavor become a vital part of your holiday experience.

Outdoor Adventures

Snorkeling and Diving

Okinawa has some of the most beautiful underwater setting in the world, making it a snorkeling and diving paradise. The Blue Cave and the Kerama Islands are two must-see places for an extraordinary underwater experience.

1. **Blue Cave**

The Blue Cave, located on Okinawa's main island, is a captivating underwater grotto known for its ethereal azure radiance. The sunlight passing through the water creates an enchanting blue hue that illuminates the cave, giving it its name. You'll be greeted by bright coral formations and an abundance of marine life as you embark on your snorkeling or diving excursion here.

The Blue Cave's crystal-clear waters offer great vision, allowing divers to explore the minute nuances of the underwater environment. The area is home to schools of tropical species, including vibrant reef fish and curious sea turtles, creating an enthralling aquatic habitat. The diving spots surrounding the Blue Cave cater to divers of all skill levels, making it a perfect location for both novice and experienced divers.

Consider visiting early in the morning, when sunlight penetrates the water, creating a dreamlike environment within the cave. Several local operators provide guided tours as well as equipment rental, assuring a safe and fun exploration of this natural beauty.

2. Kerama Islands

The Kerama Islands island group, which consists of over 20 islands, is a haven for marine biodiversity and is located just a short boat trip from Okinawa's main island. The immaculate coral reefs that encircle the Kerama Islands are a diver's dream, overflowing with a rainbow of coral formations and marine creatures.

One of the Kerama Islands, Zamami Island, is particularly known for its numerous diving spots, which appeal to both beginners and advanced divers. The pure waters here provide up to 40 meters of visibility, affording an unsurpassed glimpse of the vivid undersea world. Snorkelers will enjoy the shallow reefs, where colorful fish and coral formations may be seen from the water's surface.

Aside from the underwater splendor, the Kerama Islands provide a peaceful respite from the crowded mainland. The attraction of the underwater realm is complemented by white sandy beaches and lush green surroundings, making it an ideal location for anyone seeking a perfect balance of adventure and relaxation.

On Zamami Island, local dive operators offer guided trips to ensure that you get the most out of your underwater exploration while following to responsible diving techniques. Whether you're a beginner or a seasoned diver, the Kerama Islands will provide you with an immersive and awe-inspiring experience that will certainly leave you with lasting memories.

Okinawa's Blue Cave and the Kerama Islands offer unparalleled snorkeling and diving opportunities. These places are a must-see for anybody wishing to experience the treasures that lie beneath the East China Sea's surface, thanks to its teeming marine life, crystal-clear waters, and unique underwater landscapes.

Hiking and Nature Trails

1. **Yambaru National Park**

Yambaru National Park, located in the northernmost parts of Okinawa, is a tribute to the island's pristine natural splendor. This park provides an immersive experience in the center of lush foliage and various ecosystems for hikers and nature lovers alike. The park is large, with deep forests, crystal-clear streams, and unusual flora and wildlife.

Yambaru National Park's hiking paths accommodate to a range of skill levels, from leisurely strolls to more difficult excursions. One of the attractions is the Yanbaru Subtropical Forest Trail, where hikers may marvel at the rich array of plant life, including rare orchids and towering banyan trees. Keep an ear out for the peculiar sounds of the Okinawa rail, a local bird.

The Mount Yonaha Trail provides a hard trek with a rewarding sight of the surrounding countryside from the peak for a more panoramic view. It's an excellent location for taking amazing photos of the Okinawan nature.

2. Okinawa Honto Hiking Trails

Hiking paths on Okinawa Honto, the major island, combine cultural richness with natural grandeur. You'll come across a unique combination of Okinawan tradition and stunning landscapes as you hike these trails.

The Cape Manzamo seaside Trail is a must-see for anyone looking for a seaside hiking adventure. The walk travels along the cliffs and provides breathtaking views of the East China Sea. Capture the sunset's vivid colors for an unforgettable memory.

If you want to learn more about Okinawa's history, the Nakagusuku Castle Hiking Trail takes you past historic ruins and terraced landscapes. The route allows visitors to engage with the island's rich cultural heritage while also engaging in physical activity.

The Okinawa Kaigan Quasi-National Park offers pathways that lead to hidden beaches and isolated coves for a pleasant change of scenery. Hikers can take a break from the trails to cool down in the clear waters or simply relax in the lovely surroundings.

Finally, Okinawa's hiking paths provide a variety of experiences, ranging from the untamed nature of Yambaru National Park to the culturally rich landscapes of Okinawa Honto. Whether you're an ardent hiker or a casual nature lover, these routes provide a genuine connection to Okinawa's beauty, making your journey unique.

Events and Festivals

Naha Matsuri

This colorful festival is deeply steeped in the island's distinctive traditions and is a must-see for anybody interested in immersing themselves in the local culture.

Naha Matsuri is held in early May and lasts several days, exhibiting a mix of traditional Okinawan customs and modern festivities. The Grand Parade, a stunning parade that winds through the streets of Naha, is the festival's major attraction. Consider bright floats with complex decorations, traditional Okinawan music filling the air, and locals dressed in vibrant costumes performing traditional dances. The intensity and passion are obvious, providing fans with an amazing experience.

The celebration of Okinawa's distinct cultural history is an important component of Naha Matsuri. Eisa dances are a compelling showcase of the island's rhythmic and lyrical traditions, performed with taiko drums and sanshin instruments. During the festival, visitors may also see exciting demonstrations and performances of the Okinawan martial art of Karate.

The festival grounds are a hive of activity, with a broad choice of food stalls serving local delicacies. Naha Matsuri is a feast for the senses, with everything from savory Okinawan soba noodles to tantalizingly fresh fish. It's an excellent opportunity to sample Okinawa's particular cuisine choices while taking in the joyful ambiance.

For those looking for a more hands-on experience, the festival frequently hosts workshops and exhibitions where visitors may try their hand at traditional crafts like Bingata dyeing or learn the complicated technique of making Shisa, the iconic Okinawan lion-like guardian statues.

It is best to plan ahead of time to make the most of your Naha Matsuri experience. Check the festival schedule for particular event dates and timings, and consider booking lodgings in Naha to ensure you're close to the action.

Naha Matsuri is, in essence, a celebration of Okinawa's rich cultural fabric, a compelling blend of past and present that makes a lasting effect on everyone who engage in its joyful atmosphere. Immerse yourself in the brilliant colors, sounds, and flavors of this one-of-a-kind festival, and you'll definitely develop a better understanding for Okinawa's vibrant character.

Shurijo Castle Festival

The Shurijo Castle Festival is a dynamic event profoundly rooted in Okinawan culture, providing visitors with a unique peek into this enchanting island's rich traditions. This yearly celebration in Okinawa City recognizes the historical significance of Shurijo Castle, a UNESCO World Heritage Site.

The celebrations usually begin with a colorful parade that includes traditional Ryukyuan costumes, spectacular drum performances, and the rhythmic sounds of the sanshin, a three-stringed Okinawan instrument. The vibrant procession moves through the streets, creating an amazing ambiance that enchants both locals and tourists.

The Eisa dance competition, where several dance troupes display their skills in this frenetic and vibrant traditional dance, is one of the festival highlights. The Eisa dance, which incorporates aspects of history, folklore, and community spirit, is not just a visual show but also a powerful assertion of Okinawa's unique cultural identity.

Numerous food stalls flank the festival grounds, offering a delightful selection of Okinawan cuisine to visitors wishing to immerse themselves in the festival's environment. The festival offers a culinary trip that matches the cultural experience, with savory foods like Okinawa soba and goya champuru to sweet sweets like beni-imo tarts.

The Shurijo Castle Festival frequently includes seminars and demonstrations where attendees can try their hand at traditional crafts or learn the delicate steps of the Eisa dance, in addition to entertainment and culinary delights. This hands-on approach allows tourists to actively engage with Okinawa's cultural history, resulting in lasting memories of their visit.

The festival takes on a mystical quality as the sun sets, with the Shurijo Castle lighted in vivid hues, creating a stunning background for the evening's events. The castle grounds become a hive of activity, with live music performances, traditional ceremonies, and a spectacular fireworks show that lights up the night sky, capping off the event in style.

In essence, the Shurijo Castle Festival is more than just a festival; it is a celebration of Okinawa's history and present, a fusion of tradition and modernity that leaves a lasting effect on everyone who have the opportunity to witness it. Whether you're a history buff, a foodie, or simply looking for an unforgettable cultural experience, the Shurijo Castle Festival is a must-see event that highlights Okinawa's heart and soul.

Orion Beer Festival

The Okinawan calendar's most anticipated event, the Orion Beer Festival, has its roots in the island's deep affinity with Orion beer, a local favorite crafted with precision and devotion. The event honors this unique beverage by bringing together locals and visitors in a joyful celebration of Okinawan identity.

The festival takes place in a lively outdoor setting against the backdrop of Okinawa's gorgeous scenery, creating an inviting ambiance that resonates with the island's friendly hospitality. The captivating strains of traditional Okinawan music fill the air, blending well with the clinking of beer glasses.

The opportunity to learn about brewing from Orion's professional brewers is at the core of the event. Participate in interactive exhibits that reveal the painstaking process of creating the perfect Orion beer, from selecting the finest ingredients to the meticulous brewing procedures perfected over generations.

Indulge your senses in a culinary adventure that reflects Okinawa's rich gourmet terrain. Local vendors serve a delectable selection of meals ranging from traditional Okinawan delicacies to cosmopolitan flavors, each carefully crafted to compliment the deep, malty tones of Orion beer.

The Orion Beer Festival is more than just a beer festival; it is also a celebration of Okinawan arts and entertainment. Experience the island's cultural energy through spectacular performances of traditional dance, taiko drumming, and live music.

The festival's capacity to bring people together is one of its distinguishing features. Join the locals in a communal toast, share stories, and make new acquaintances in a welcoming environment. The celebration represents Okinawa's inclusive character, welcoming anyone to participate in the festivities.

Plan your visit during the festival dates, which are normally held during the lively summer months. For the most up-to-date information, including event schedules, participating brewers, and any special attractions, visit the festival's official website.

The Orion Beer Festival is more than just a beer festival; it's a celebration of Okinawa's soul, a mix of tradition and modernity, and a chance to sample the island's distinct flavors. So come participate in the fun, raise your glass, and immerse yourself in the heady combination of Orion beer and Okinawan hospitality that distinguishes this amazing celebration.

Weather and Climate

Spring (March-May): Spring brings a pleasant combination of warm temperatures and blossoming greenery. During this season, the average temperature ranges from 20 to 25 degrees Celsius (68 to 77 degrees Fahrenheit). It's an excellent time to discover Okinawa's natural splendor, from cherry blossoms to bright coral reefs.

Summer (June to August): Prepare for the Okinawan summer, which is distinguished by hot and humid weather. Temperatures might reach 30 degrees Celsius (86 degrees Fahrenheit). This time of year is ideal for beachgoers, with crystal-clear waters and cool ocean breezes providing welcome relief from the heat.

Autumn (September to November): As summer transitions to autumn, temperatures gradually cool down, ranging from 25 to 30 degrees Celsius (77 to 86 degrees Fahrenheit). This time of year is ideal for outdoor activities and cultural exploration. As you go across the island, keep an eye out for the brilliant colors of fall foliage.

Winter (December to February): Compared to mainland Japan, Okinawa's winter is mild, with temperatures ranging from 15 to 20 degrees Celsius (59 to 68 degrees Fahrenheit). While it may not be beach weather, winter in Okinawa provides a comfortable environment for tourism and allows you to see the island's unique cultural offerings.

Okinawa has a separate rainy season known as the "Tsuyu" or plum rain season, which lasts from early May until mid-June. Increased rainfall is expected during this time period, so pack appropriately. Don't let the rain dampen your mood, though; the lush landscapes come alive, creating a gorgeous environment.

Okinawa's typhoon season normally lasts from June to November, with the largest probability of typhoons happening in August and September. While the chances of a direct strike are minimal, it's a good idea to stay up to date on weather forecasts and be prepared to adjust your travel plans if necessary.

Throughout the year, Okinawa's weather and climate provide a broad range of experiences. Whether you enjoy the sun, environment, or culture, Okinawa has something for you in every season.

Get your FREE book

Please visit https://tinyurl.com/travel-with-jeffery for additional resources and to engage with my newsletter.

I also want to reward you for purchasing my book. To get the reward which is a travel planner; kindly click on this link below or open the link on your browser.

https://tinyurl.com/travel-with-jeffery

I hope you love the travel planner!

Best Times to Visit

What is the ideal time to visit Okinawa? Okinawa is officially a year-round destination; however, my firsthand experience contradicts this. While my preliminary research indicated that early February was near the top of the list of best times to visit Okinawa, the conditions I met were appalling—thick clouds, heavy rain, howling wind, and temperatures ranging from 3o to 5oC. As a result, I can't advocate anyone visiting Okinawa between November and March, despite the fact that things to do in Okinawa in March are theoretically similar to what you could do in May or September.

On the other hand, because so of much of what to do in Okinawa is done outdoors, and because the archipelago also has a long monsoon and typhoon season between June and October, this is not an ideal time to visit Okinawa, at least not on paper. In actuality, I've discovered that rain in Okinawa comes and passes swiftly throughout the Japanese summer; other from that, April and May are generally good months to visit Okinawa. My most recent trip to Okinawa was in September, and aside from some haze on Tokashiki island, the weather was wonderful.

Currency and Payment Methods

Understanding the local currency and payment options is critical when going on your Okinawa vacation to ensure a smooth and happy experience. Okinawa is a part of Japan, hence its official currency is the Japanese Yen (JPY).

It's a good idea to exchange some dollars into Japanese Yen before visiting this gorgeous island. While major credit cards are commonly accepted in tourist regions, having cash on hand is useful in more rural spots or local markets. Currency exchange is simple at airports, banks, and authorized currency exchange agencies.

Okinawa has a well-developed infrastructure, and ATMs can be found in most urban locations. It is, however, critical to check that your credit or debit card is international compatible. Visa and Mastercard are usually accepted, however it's a good idea to notify your bank about your vacation dates to avoid any potential card transaction complications.

While credit cards are useful, cash is still king in Okinawa, particularly at smaller shops, local markets, and traditional restaurants. It's a good idea to keep some cash on hand for these occasions. Many traditional Ryokans (inns) and local eateries may request cash payments.

Okinawa, like the rest of Japan, has embraced mobile payments. Suica, Pasmo, and IC cards are popular services that can be used for public transportation, vending machines, and even at some retailers. However, it should be noted that these are more common in mainland Japan, and their use may be limited on Okinawa.

Tipping is not customary in Japan, including Okinawa. The total experience already includes exceptional service, and tipping may even be considered disrespectful. It is usually more polite to express gratitude by word.

Consider downloading translation applications to help you bridge language barriers during transactions to improve your payment experience. While English is commonly spoken in tourist areas, knowing a few simple Japanese words can make your encounters more enjoyable.

A well-prepared journey to Okinawa in terms of currency and payment methods will surely help to a smooth and delightful experience. Embrace the island's distinct charm, experience its cultural riches, and savor every minute knowing that the practicalities are fully under control.

Health and Safety Information

Here are some crucial health and safety advice for your Okinawa travel experience to ensure a safe and pleasurable journey.

1. Sun Protection:

Okinawa is blessed with plenty of sunshine, so bring a high-SPF sunscreen with you. Apply it liberally, especially if you intend to spend time outside, whether exploring Shurijo Castle or relaxing on the gorgeous Katsuren Peninsula beaches.

2. Hydration:

Okinawa's subtropical climate means it can get fairly hot and humid. Drink plenty of water throughout the day to stay hydrated. Consider carrying a reusable water bottle to reduce plastic waste and guarantee you always have access to water.

3. Local Cuisine:

Enjoy Okinawa's unique culinary delights, but keep food safety in mind. Enjoy the well-known Okinawan longevity diet, which is high in veggies and tofu. Make certain that fish and meat items are adequately cooked, and choose reputed restaurants for your dining experiences.

4. Mosquito Protection:

While Okinawa is largely pest-free, it is recommended that you bring mosquito repellent, especially if you want to visit the lush forests or the Okinawa World amusement park. Long sleeves and slacks in the evening can also give an extra layer of protection.

5. Emergency Services

Save local emergency phone numbers in your phone and know where the nearest medical facilities are. Okinawa has superb healthcare, but it's always a good idea to be prepared. For optimal conversation, learn basic Japanese phrases or use translation tools.

6. Respect Local Customs:

Okinawa is a distinct fusion of Japanese and Ryukyuan cultures. Respect local customs and traditions, such as bowing as a politeness symbol. To ensure a peaceful encounter with the natives, become acquainted with fundamental etiquette.

7. COVID-19 Considerations:

Check the most recent COVID-19 travel advisories and health guidelines. Follow any quarantine or testing procedures that have been established, and be prepared with the relevant documentation. Keep up to date on local health protocols to ensure a safe and responsible visit.

8. Beach Safety:

The gorgeous beaches of Okinawa are a big draw. Swim in designated places, avoid strong currents, and heed any posted cautions. Always keep an eye on children and, if necessary, employ floating devices.

9. Transportation Safety:

Prioritize transportation safety when exploring Naha's lively marketplaces or trekking to the secluded islands. Follow traffic laws, cross at specified crosswalks, and exercise caution when hiring scooters or bicycles.

10. Travel Insurance:

Consider purchasing comprehensive travel insurance that includes coverage for medical emergencies, trip cancellations, and other unforeseen circumstances. It gives you peace of mind and financial security in the event of an unforeseen event.

You'll be well-prepared to explore Okinawa's attractions safely if you keep these health and safety guidelines in mind. In this picturesque destination, embrace the beauty of the islands, immerse yourself in the local culture, and make memorable experiences.

Entertainment and Nightlife

Okinawa's entertainment and nightlife scene provides a new dimension to the island experience. As the sun sets over this tropical paradise, a plethora of alternatives await visitors looking to immerse themselves in Okinawa's throbbing beat after dark.

Okinawa's entertainment culture is profoundly rooted in the island's own cultural heritage. Immerse yourself in the island's rich traditions by seeing enthralling Eisa performances, a dynamic drum dance that originated in Okinawa. These vibrant performances, complemented by bright costumes and rhythmic sounds, transport viewers to a bygone period, providing an enthralling peek into the island's cultural essence.

No trip to Okinawa's nightlife would be complete without delving into the island's ardent love affair with karaoke. Step into one of the colorful karaoke bars, where locals and tourists alike sing along to J-pop, traditional Okinawan folk songs, and international favorites. Immerse yourself in the contagious atmosphere of a karaoke room, making memories that will last long after the music has faded.

Okinawa's nightlife is tightly intertwined into its culinary environment for anyone looking for a gastronomic journey. Izakayas, traditional Japanese bars, entice with wonderful foods and locally made awamori, Okinawa's peculiar rice spirit. Participate in the age-old practice of "tachinomi" (standing bars), creating a convivial environment where strangers become friends over shared plates and laughs.

Okinawa's coastline attractiveness takes center stage as the night progresses. The rhythmic murmur of coastal waves harmonizes with live music at beachfront bars and cafes, creating an intimate ambiance under the starlit sky. While relaxing in the pleasant sea breeze, sip tropical cocktails and sample Okinawa's renowned Orion beer.

Okinawa's electronic music culture pulses through the veins of its nightlife for those looking for a more current groove. After dark, trendy clubs and coastal dance festivals come alive with local and international DJs. Immerse yourself in the mesmerizing beats as neon lights reflect off the swaying masses, creating an electric mood that reflects the island's modern attitude.

The entertainment and nightlife of Okinawa go beyond regular venues. Discover the island's bustling night markets, where local craftsmen display their wares, street performers enchant audiences, and the enticing aroma of street cuisine fills the air. Immerse yourself in the exuberant atmosphere of cultural events, making unforgettable memories against the stunning nightscape of Okinawa.

Okinawa's entertainment and nightlife weave a fascinating fabric of heritage and modernity. Whether you're captivated by the rhythmic beats of traditional performances, harmonizing in a vibrant karaoke bar, relishing local specialties in an izakaya, or dancing beneath the stars at a beachside soirée, Okinawa provides an unrivaled nocturnal journey. Surrender to the beauty of Okinawa's nights as the island transforms from dusk to night, where every moment is a celebration of life, culture, and the simple joy of being in this tropical paradise.

Conclusion

Okinawa is a jewel in the broad tapestry of travel destinations, offering a unique blend of rich cultural heritage, magnificent natural beauty, and a tranquil getaway from contemporary life.

The charm of Okinawa resides not just in its beautiful beaches, historical landmarks, and busy markets, but also in the profound sense of harmony that pervades the islands. Each nook of Okinawa whispers stories of tenacity, history, and the continuing spirit of its residents, from the old Shurijo Castle to the tranquil coastlines of Katsuren Peninsula.

The local cuisine, a delectable fusion of Chinese, Japanese, and Southeast Asian influences, adds another element to the Okinawan experience. Savoring the distinct aromas of Goya Champuru or indulging in a feast of Okinawa soba noodles is a cultural experience that ties you to the very core of the islands.

Furthermore, the Okinawan way of life, which is frequently cited as one of the secrets to their longevity, inspires tourists to slow down, appreciate the present moment, and find delight in simplicity.

In essence, Okinawa entices visitors with the promise of an out-of-the-ordinary experience. It's a place where the past and present collide, where nature and culture coexist, and where the spirit of "island time" beckons you to embrace a slower, more meaningful way of life.

Thank you for purchasing this guide; I wish you a memorable experience.

Printed in Great Britain
by Amazon